Improve Your Presentation Skills in One Hour

*Practical Tips for
In-Person or Remote Presentations*

By Jason Chase

© 2020, Nineteen LLC. All rights reserved.

Table of Contents

ONE HOUR TO READ THE BOOK. ONE WEEK TO DRAMATICALLY IMPROVE YOUR PRESENTATION SKILLS.   4

CHAPTER 1 KNOW AND ORGANIZE YOUR MATERIAL   7

CHAPTER 2 KNOWING YOUR AUDIENCE IMPROVES YOUR OUTPUT   11

CHAPTER 3 LEARN FROM OTHERS   13

CHAPTER 4 VISUALIZE SUCCESS!   15

CHAPTER 5 NARROW THE SCOPE OF YOUR MATERIAL   17

CHAPTER 6 REHEARSE AND THEN REHEARSE AGAIN   21

CHAPTER 7 FIVE MINUTES OF ADVANCED PREP ON THE DAY OF THE PRESENTATION   25

CHAPTER 8 THE POINT OF NO RETURN: DELIVERING YOUR PRESENTATION   28

CHAPTER 9 BRINGING IT ALL TOGETHER   31

One Hour to Read the Book.
One Week to Dramatically Improve Your Presentation Skills.

Delivering a presentation is so commonplace in today's society that it's almost unavoidable. From the small classroom reports delivered in school to the regular meeting presentations at work, presenting all boils down to one thing: Sharing information. But it's more than just giving a draggy, memorized speech to others. A good presentation depends both on matter (the quality of the material) and on manner (the quality of the delivery).

This book is intentionally brief. You can read the whole thing in one hour. This book will give you the practical knowhow to hone your skills and improve your presentations—whether you deliver them in-person or remotely. But keep in mind, although you can read this book in one hour, you need to do some work to practice the skills. Just like playing a musical instrument or a sport, presenting takes practice. You will improve with each tip you incorporate.

> A good presentation depends both on matter (the quality of the material) and on manner (the quality of the delivery).

Most of us face fear when giving a presentation. That's normal. We get immeasurably nervous at the thought of addressing a large amount of people—whether standing in front of them or presenting over video conference call—all eyes focused only on us. That amount of attention is enough to make us shrink and feel like all our mistakes will be noticed, pointed out, and laughed at. On the other hand, we're also afraid that no one will pay any attention if we are boring. It feels like a situation where there is no way to win. Damned if you do, damned if you don't.

This book will help you take control of that fear.

Learning to be a good presenter actually has some awesome perks to it! Aside from the general improvement of speaking skills that *everyone* can benefit from, knowing that we are capable of delivering an excellent presentation is a huge boost to our confidence. It also opens up opportunities for us. You never know the next time you have a person in your audience who shares your name with others because he or she was impressed with not only what you said, but also how you said it.

This book will help you get noticed because of your confident presentation skills.

This book will give you the basic tips on how to improve your presentation skills. From pre-presentation preparations that start from the time you decide to give a presentation, all the way to those moments when you find yourself addressing an audience, there's always something you can work on to deliver the best material in the best way possible. Individually, the tips you'll find here are just small boosts to your skills, but when you put them all together, you will find yourself on your way to becoming a more polished speaker!

This book will guide you step-by-step through the proper process to prepare for and deliver an excellent presentation.

So, let's get started.

Chapter 1
Know and Organize Your Material

A speaker is a giver. You cannot give what you do not have. You cannot give a presentation about quantum physics if you do not have any idea about how it works or what it even is. Okay, so maybe you will not be talking about complicated topics like quantum physics; in fact, you will find that a lot of the popular presentations or speeches (try looking them up on YouTube) have topics that almost anyone can relate to: how to work smarter, how to manage your finances better, how to keep going in the face of adversity, you get the idea. The point is, no matter how simple or complicated your topic of choice will be, the only way you will deliver a quality presentation is if you do your research and know your material way before you step in front of the audience.

Your role on stage is to help your listeners learn from you. There will be something in that room that only you have, and the goal is to let everyone else have it too by the time you are done. That is pretty much the essence of presenting or public speaking: the ideas in your mind should flow into the minds of those before you, and the audience will learn something from you only if you yourself know what you are talking about.

Now you might be thinking, "Sounds like I need heavy credentials to be able to give something that's worth listening to." The good news is that no, you don't need to be a CEO of a Silicon Valley tech company to give a talk about the next innovations in computer technology. Nor do you need to be one of the top Wall Street traders to be able to give a worthy talk about stocks and investments. Sure, it would be nice to be an expert on something so you can be sure about what you are talking about, but unless you are defending your doctoral dissertation before a panel of established authorities on the subject, you just need to know and deliver something that the average member of the audience does not know. We'll tackle more of this in the next chapter, but the point is, you don't have to be an expert on the topic you'll be speaking about, but you definitely need to do your research.

> The initial "product" you come up with will look like a mosaic that was roughly stitched together, which has to be polished and smoothed to make the seams invisible.

After you feel that you are prepared with your internal knowledge of the material, it is time to make sure the content flows smoothly from one part to another. The goal here is to make it appear that the whole thing was made and will be spoken by only one person. Definitely, throughout the course of your "scriptwriting," you will gather information from multiple sources including your own base knowledge. The initial "product" you come up with will look like a mosaic that was roughly stitched together, which has to be polished and smoothed to make the seams invisible.

Look at the outline of your presentation. Do the individual parts transition smoothly from and to one another? Transitions can be tricky. Make sure that each part ends in a sort-of introduction to the next part so that when you proceed to the next one, the audience is not too jarred by the change. Remember, unless you were specifically chosen to present on two different topics, you want to make sure that you present cohesive material, not disparate materials presented one after another. Going back to the mosaic example, you should see the different components when you look at your presentation closely, but when you move back and zoom out, you will see one big coherent picture.

Find ways to bring the material to life for the audience. I have learned this firsthand. As a market researcher, I share a lot of data with my clients. Some of it can be hard for the audience to consume. I have to bring it to life. The best way to do that with the material I share is to sprinkle stories into the mix—stories from the people I have interviewed. Stories stick with the audience. So, they have to be relevant to the narrative of the presentation. The audience will share stories with others when they leave the presentation. So, find ways to bring the material to life.

> Your introduction will make or break your presentation, so work on that crucial first minute.

When you are finally pleased with your overall output, then is the time to work on the introduction. It might sound counterintuitive, I know. Why save preparing the introduction for the last part of the creative process? Well, you want your introduction to be catchy: You have to capture your audience's attention within the first minute, and it's even better if you get it in the first 30 seconds. For that to happen, you will need to have a deep understanding of your presentation as a whole, which you gain after working on the bigger picture and understanding the key points of your material—transitions and small details included.

Never start with something basic like, "Today, I will be speaking about…." Make it different and catchy. Ask a rhetorical question. Give a motivational quote. Tell a story. You can even try starting with something that *seems* totally unrelated, but make sure to tie it into your presentation eventually. Remember, a strong intro ensures your audience stays listening throughout your entire presentation, whether it lasts for five minutes or 10 minutes. Your introduction will make or break your presentation, so work on that crucial first minute.

Chapter 2
Knowing Your Audience
Improves Your Output

Are you speaking to undergraduates who are only attending because of a class requirement? Or maybe you're speaking at an academic conference filled with experts and authorities in an industry. Perhaps you were just instructed to deliver a report on your company's sales for the past quarter. Regardless, knowing your audience is just as important as knowing your topic. Different people process information in different ways: academic conference audiences might be able to tolerate (and even expect!) a presentation filled with technical jargon, but speak that way to high school students or college kids and you might find your audience is listening to something or someone other than you. Match the semantics of your audience.

An important thing to keep in mind when delivering a presentation is that you are presenting for your audience, not for yourself. You're not there to pad your resume or just to improve your speaking skills (although they are certainly a nice bonus), but you are there to share what you know, that only *you* in that room know. Align your presentation with this in mind. If you're hesitating over a particular aspect of delivery, such as wording or even calculated gestures, just ask yourself, "What kind of presentation will work best for *this* audience so that they are able to absorb what I am going to say in the best way possible?"

> Knowing your audience is just as important as knowing your topic.

Public speaking coaches even recommend sending questionnaires in advance to some of the audience members. This works especially well for larger events. If you are going to speak before a conference with a large audience, try to prepare some questionnaires, blend in with the crowd before the event officially starts, and get them to answer a just few questions. If you don't have the resources to prepare dozens of questionnaires, you can just speak with a few attendees. Get a feel for what your audience is like by talking to a few of them. If you are confident that you can make small adjustments to your presentation a few minutes before your scheduled time, you can drastically improve your speech because the audience will be able to better connect with you. When you eventually get up there and begin, seeing a more engaged audience can be a huge confidence boost!

Find ways to genuinely connect with your audience. The important word in that sentence is "genuinely." The best way to do this is to share part of yourself with your audience. Some presenters use humor or jokes. I'm not a joke guy. My delivery is all wrong. If I try to force it, it falls flat. But I am a storyteller. When I can find a way to infuse a relevant story about my life into my material, then the connection is palpable.

Chapter 3
Learn from Others

Regardless of how skilled you are or think you are, you can always learn something from others who are more experienced. Public speaking is a craft, and there are masters out there.

Many presenters might feel this tip is applicable only for those who are just beginning to step into the vast world of public speaking. But even polished presenters can learn something from other presenters—so please don't skip it. Contact someone who has more presenting experience than you and ask for their general tips. Even better, ask them if you can practice your whole presentation in front of them (I'm assuming you already have it prepared if you've read this book's chapters in sequence) and have them point out the areas where you can improve.

> A mentor can point out a few nervous habits to you and, thus, can drastically improve your performance.

The less experienced we are, the less likely we are aware of the areas where we can improve, especially in subtle ways. Nervous people will have tics that they do not know they are doing but are totally visible to everyone else. Perhaps you look to the side way too often, or you unconsciously keep touching your face or fidget with your hands. Maybe you say certain words or phrases a little too often. I would know. The first time I tried to deliver a presentation, one of the first comments I received was that I said "now" at the start of almost every sentence. It sounded natural to me (or so I thought), but to everyone who listened, it was really distracting! Trust me, there are a lot of things that reveal our nervousness and anxiety that we cannot spot on our own, precisely because we are too nervous to notice. A mentor can point out a few nervous habits to you and, thus, can drastically improve your performance.

Have you ever heard of the Toastmasters group? They are an international organization dedicated to improving the public speaking skills of their members. Their name comes from the fact that people who give a toast at social events usually have to deliver a quick speech that lasts around a minute or so. Don't be fooled by the name, though. They're engaged in all forms of public speaking training—from short toasts to full-on reports and presentations! You might want to check your community to see if you have a local Toastmasters club in your area. It could prove to be time and energy well spent.

Regardless of how you plan to learn from others, the most crucial thing to get is feedback—immediate feedback that you can use to correct any bad habits you may have ingrained into your system and add new tricks to your delivery so you can be a compelling speaker from start to finish.

Chapter 4
Visualize Success!

When we imagine a positive outcome, it's more likely to play out the way we envision. Visualize yourself in the setting where you will be making your presentation, whether it's a stage, a small office, or the raised platform in front of your classroom. Get used to the thought of having people look at you from the very start. The more nervous you are in front of others, the earlier you should start getting yourself used to this.

The most important thing to visualize, however, is a picture of yourself delivering point after point smoothly and totally nailing that presentation so that you receive thunderous applause! When we visualize ourselves succeeding, the usual feeling that follows is happiness. We imagine ourselves in a place of success and it feels good. But do not make the mistake that visualization is all that it takes to improve. Making yourself feel good with mental images of success should always be followed by the actions that actually *help you* realize success.

> Get used to the thought of having people look at you from the very start.

When you imagine yourself succeeding at a goal, ask yourself, "Is there anything I should be doing right now to make this image closer to reality?" List everything that you should be doing and start incorporating them ASAP! You should also ask yourself, "Are there things I am doing that hinder me from attaining that success?" Reflect upon these and work on removing them from your style.

See, visualization is both an underestimated and overestimated tool—not just for improving your presentation skills, but for becoming successful in your general endeavors. It's underestimated because most people don't bother with it, thinking it is too abstract or it does not bring any tangible results. But for those who use it, they also tend to overestimate it because they settle for just imagining the results without actually working to get those results.

Visualization should always go hand-in-hand with other actions, like preparation and practice. If you can add *proper* visualization to your list of things to do for improvement, you will notice massive changes not only in your progress, but also in your confidence, which I'd argue goes an even longer way for you as a whole.

Chapter 5
Narrow the Scope of Your Material

Another crucial part of preparation that is just as important as knowing what to put into your presentation is knowing what *not* to put in. In other words, learn how to trim your presentation to just the key essentials!

Have you ever attended a talk that sounded really interesting for the first few minutes but then after a while you noticed that the speaker is meandering all over the place? It seems like he doesn't know what he wants to talk about exactly. In his desire to tackle a lot of subtopics that he thinks are "essential," he fails to notice that he is no longer talking about anything in depth!

Now, I can't give you a specific list of things that should be excluded from your presentation; after all, what is and what is not essential varies widely from topic to topic. There is no hard and fast checklist that works for every topic. But a good place to start is by asking yourself yet another question, "Will my presentation still make sense if I remove this point?" If your speech can stand completely, even if you remove a part or two, then those parts are probably unnecessary and can even detract from the main topic. As the creator of your own outline, you will probably think that all the parts you put in are necessary for the audience to truly understand what you are talking about, but more often than not, that is not really the case. In most instances, there are always things that you can and should trim out. In the world of writing, we call this "killing your darlings." You feel attached to them, but you need to view them with an objective eye. The best approach is to draft your initial outline, sit on it for a day or two (don't even review or look at it during this time), and then try to sit down and trim it. The reviewing and trimming process requires fresh eyes, and you will probably not find much success when you try to cut your material right after drafting it.

> The maximum time allotted is also usually an indicator of the level of detail that the audience expects from you.

When you are invited to deliver a presentation, you will never be given an unlimited amount of time to present. If you are speaking at an event, the organizers will assign you a set amount of time in which to deliver your presentation. You cannot exceed this because there are other activities lined up for the day and if you spend too much time on your segment, you will ruin the event's meticulously planned schedule. So, when receiving the invitation to speak, be sure to find out the maximum time you have been given to deliver. This maximum time allotted is also usually an indicator of the level of detail that the audience expects from you. If you are given a five-minute timeframe, people will usually expect an overview with a few key details. They will not expect a crammed dissertation, but they will expect more or less a quick rundown of your topic with specific information sprinkled in between.

On the other side of the spectrum, if you are given 30 minutes, people will expect a slower pace and more attention to detail from you. You could probably afford to add in a few slightly related subtopics in these longer presentations. The time limit is also a good indicator of the rough *minimum* you have to meet, although there usually is not a specific minimum time indicated. If you have 15 minutes to present and your presentation is done after only 4-5 minutes, maybe you are not providing as much detail as the occasion calls for and you will likely leave the audience unsatisfied with the material. Knowing how much time you have to speak is a very important step of the process, so you have an exact idea of how much information to deliver. A presentation that meets the expectations of the audience as to the level of depth of information will leave them feeling good about attending and will leave you feeling good about your performance. You might even have a VIP in the audience recommend you for bigger opportunities if she is impressed with your presentation.

People are visual creatures, and this is critical when talking about technical topics. If you plan to use a slideshow, use visuals to accompany your presentation as best as you can. Many newbie presenters make the mistake of loading too many words on their slides; worse, they end up reading the paragraphs they are presenting which turns a presentation into a monotonous one-man reading session. If you plan to use a slideshow, remember that it should *accompany, complement, and enhance* the spoken part of your presentation. For example, if you will be talking about budgets and sales targets, you might want to put charts and graphs on your slides so that the audience can better follow you. If they see nothing but words and numbers on the wall, and *also hear* words and numbers from you, you can expect them to lose track of the topic a few moments into your presentation. Keep it visual, and if you need to use words on your slides, limit them to headings and bullet points of the most important parts of your topics.

> If you plan to use a slideshow, remember that it should accompany, complement, and enhance the spoken part of your presentation.

Trimming and adjusting the length of your presentation does not necessarily mean that you should just remove the finer details. That would be an oversimplified approach to the editing process that can leave you with an even worse output than when you started. Rather, think of the trimming process as a way to keep your entire presentation intact with the topic you were given, or as a way to make sure that you are on track and are consistently engaging the audience with the essentials.

Chapter 6
Rehearse and then Rehearse Again

One practice session is not enough. Athletes and musicians practice for hours on end, so the same principle applies to public speaking. Rehearsing is a way for you to see how you will perform on the actual day. If there is a possibility you might make mistakes, fumble, or fidget during the real performance, it would be better for you to make them in practice so you will not make them on stage. The goal of practice is to remove bad habits and reinforce or improve good habits. This is your chance to figure out phrasing of your key points, to identify the ideal sequence to tell your stories with punch, to determine where you should pause for emphasis, and to practice pacing—where does your audience want you to move quickly versus where do they want you to spend more time? You will spot numerous errors during the first practice session. That's okay. Work on them and practice *again* so you can uncover additional slips that you might have missed because previous glaring mistakes were taking up too much of the spotlight. This is going to be the most repetitive part of preparation, but do not take "repetitiveness" too literally; if you keep making the same mistakes and keep getting the same feedback, you may need to first address the root issue behind the mistakes.

> Unpolished presenters hate to practice. But practicing without memorizing opens the door to letting you be yourself in an uncomfortable situation.

Most people make the mistake of thinking that they can just write a speech, memorize it, and call it a day. That is absolutely NOT what you want to do. You want to appear lively and engaging, and delivering a memorized speech is exactly the opposite. Instead, you might just look and sound robotic, monotonous, and unengaging. The only place where the absolute memorization of lines is proper is in acting, where dialogue is carefully crafted to elicit specific emotions and reactions; even then, a lot of impromptu acting still happens. During your presentation, you want to give the impression that you are engaging in conversation and interacting with your audience, like you are talking to all of them individually, while collectively delivering your material. The best presentations sound conversational—even presentations on technical topics like medicine or physics. People will be actively listening to you, so do your part to individually *talk to them*.

You might think that memorizing can give you confidence because the risk of a 10-second dead air is eliminated, but there's an equally present risk of seeming too distant from the audience. David Parnell, the author of a book on the psychology of effective communication says that when an individual is too polished, "it makes them relatively inaccessible in the mind of the audience." The result is that nobody will listen to you because you will seem like you are in a world of your own, and all the effort that went into your preparation will go to waste. The common suggestion for this is to just prepare an outline of your general topics and subtopics, and then practice talking about them. If you must memorize something, limit it to your outline. Eventually, if you keep practicing properly and consistently, you will get the hang of this and you will be able to deliver all your material with just an outline in the back of your head.

Practicing is not limited to one specific presentation. Practice your speaking skills *in general,* whether at school or in your community. If you are active in your local church, there are plenty of speaking opportunities there. Remember Toastmasters? Look it up. Maybe they have events near you. Take whatever opportunity is available to practice speaking. Generally, public speaking skills carry over to presentation skills. That is why you might know someone who is a well-versed public speaker in other ways (maybe he joined debate or rhetoric contests in school), and when he is assigned to deliver a presentation, he accepts easily and delivers it naturally. When I say "practice," I mean it in a holistic way; any improvements you can make to your general speaking skills will definitely help your presentations, no matter how small.

It's not all about the speech. Practice your movement and body language too. If you do not have a mentor to help you out with immediate constructive criticism, you can do this by video recording yourself. If you feel embarrassed at the thought of watching yourself on video, remember that what you'll be watching is what the audience will be seeing. Get used to seeing yourself from an outside perspective. We are our own worst critics. There will be a lot of tiny flaws that might make you cringe, but the audience probably won't see them. Remember, it is better that *you* (and a close mentor if you have one) see your mistakes in private, rather than make them in public for everyone to see.

Unpolished presenters hate to practice. But practicing without memorizing opens the door to letting you be yourself in an uncomfortable situation. When you can be yourself, your audience will connect with you. When they connect with you, they will lean in even more to your content. This is time well invested.

Chapter 7
Five Minutes of Advanced Prep on the Day of the Presentation

Okay, it's the day that you'll be presenting. You were told that you have five minutes to prepare before it's your turn. Just before presenting, do a few exercises to prepare your mind and body. These preparation tips work whether you are standing on a stage in front of 100 people or are presenting via Zoom to five people.

Stretch your mouth and neck. When people get nervous, their muscles tense—including their voice muscles. Open and close your mouth repeatedly to stretch the muscles in your lips and face. Stretch your neck in all directions to loosen your throat. Warm your throat too. If you haven't been speaking for the past hour, go to a private place and do lip trills and warm your throat. Trust me, you do not want your confidence to leave you after you have spoken just one word because your voice suddenly cracked. Take your time to warm your vocal cords and relax your muscles.

> Put on the mantle of authority. At the moment of your presentation, remind yourself that you know more about your topic than most people in the room.

Relax your shoulders. Perhaps you've been tense all day from the moment you woke up. You might not even notice that your shoulders are pulled tight. Tense shoulders give an impression of unpreparedness or a lack of confidence. Be mindful and relax them. Stretch them. Roll them forwards and backwards. Shake your arms.

Get out of your head. Remind yourself that the audience is attending your presentation because they want to listen to what you have to say about the topic. I remember once looking into the faces of an audience as I presented. Their expressions looked stern and critical—even judgmental. They looked like they doubted the content I was delivering. My confidence was shaken during the entire presentation. A few days later, when I discussed my perception of their reaction with my mentor, she corrected me. She said, "They weren't doubting you. They were just focused on your message. The facial expression is the same." She was spot on! I know this, because I received an email that same day praising me for my presentation. So, get out of your head. Don't be too hard on yourself and don't focus on the mistakes you made in practice, thinking you'll make them again. The reality is, you're probably the harshest towards yourself. Ease up a little and remember that you've worked hard and prepared well for this.

Finally, put on the mantle of authority. At the moment of your presentation, remind yourself that you know more about your topic than most people in the room. You are the authority on your presentation. Wear that mantle and present with confidence. Generally, the audience will just take in whatever you say at face value, but this won't happen as much if you sound weak or unsure of yourself. Remember, the audience is there to learn from you, and they can't learn much if they see the speaker is uncertain whether what he's saying is correct. Have you ever heard people who are talking straight-up gibberish, but you can't help but entertain the thought that they might be right, *because they're speaking so confidently?* I'm not saying that you start throwing false information all over the place; what I'm saying is, if you can speak confidently (even if it's just fake confidence), it can and will go a long way in keeping your audience engaged and listening to you.

Chapter 8
The Point of No Return:
Delivering Your Presentation

When you stand in front of everyone, make eye contact with a few people scattered around the room as you present. A good tip from most public speakers is to pick out just a few audience members from different parts of the room and rotate eye contact between them. (I like to pick the ones who are smiling.) This can give the illusion that you are talking to the entire room, and it can also help your gaze appear focused.

Let your arms and hands hang by your side and only occasionally use them in natural gestures. Many presenters feel self-conscious about their arms and hands and then overuse them, which becomes a distraction to the audience. Use gestures in a calculated way to emphasize a point. The presenter who waves his hands from start to finish will probably be remembered as the presenter trying to take flight! But the presenter who uses hand gestures only on the emphatic parts will bring more attention to the words that come out of his mouth when his hands are also being used. Use gestures but use them sparingly and use a mixture of them. They are a good accompaniment to your presentation and can make your presentation feel more alive and natural.

> Pause between sentences. Let your audience process the information and insights that you shared.

As you speak, relax, calm down, and slow your breathing and your speaking. Pause between sentences. Let your audience process the information and insights that you shared. Keeping a controlled pace regardless makes the audience feel at ease, and more likely to keep listening to you. When you start to feel the need to rush, just remember that the goal is to get the audience to learn, whether or not you finish all of your material (but of course, make sure to practice properly to ensure that you do finish it).

Don't be afraid of dead air. If you need to pause to refer to your notes, do it. The audience understands. Rather than announcing that you've lost your place or you can't remember what you wanted to say, build anticipation instead by saying something like, "I want to read this next point because it's important and I want to make sure I get it right for you."

Expect glitches. When you've prepared both your content and your delivery, you are better able to react confidently when spur-of-the-moment surprises pop up. For example, I watched a presenter at a large conference once. He was clipping along beautifully. He had the audience eating out of his hand. He was leading up to a big reveal. And then his phone rang during his presentation. He had forgotten to silence it. Because he was so well prepared for his content and his delivery, he wasn't rattled. Without missing a beat, he said with a wink, "Hold on, I have to take this call." His reaction gave a glimpse of his humor and personality with the audience. The audience responded with laughter and warmth.

Finally, don't worry about the time limit; focus more on ensuring that the audience can process each and every word that you have said. While it's best to cover everything you prepared for, on the off chance that you feel like your time will not be enough, make sure to maintain a proper pace and speed and skip certain subtopics if you have to. Don't make the audience feel like you are rushing them. If you feel like you are about to run out of time, rushing your words and your slides will just end up with the audience not being able to understand anything which just wastes your time and theirs. It's also very jarring for a speaker to start off nice and slow but end up rushing through the end of their presentation.

Chapter 9
Bringing It All Together

Delivering a presentation before an audience, no matter how big or small, can be quite a nerve-wracking experience for many, especially the uninitiated. I've always believed that *proper* preparation is the best way to stave off nervousness and stage fright. When you walk on that stage with the knowledge that you know your material like the back of your hand, you feel more confident and sure of yourself. Just recall the times in school when your teacher asked you a question: when did you feel more confident in speaking up? When you knew about the topic or when you were clueless about the topic?

Preparation is important but take care not to overdo it and end up sounding and looking robotic. There's a reason they chose to listen to you, so make sure to meet those expectations and make your presentation sound like something worth listening to.

> Don't point out your mistakes.

No matter what happens, remember that you are your worst critic. Most of the time, the mistakes you think you are making are the ones only you notice, and the audience won't notice them unless you point them out to them. Don't do that. Don't point out your mistakes. When you have prepared your content well, they will focus on taking in the content. Knowing this, they probably will not be able to notice small, inconsequential mistakes that you thought were already addressed in practice. If you make a minor slip up on stage, carry on and act like no mistake happened. The audience is more forgiving than you think.

Finally, how you deliver is sometimes more important than what you deliver. As Lilly Walters wisely put it, "The success of your presentation will be judged not by the knowledge you send but by what the listener receives."

Now go out there and engage the world. And if you follow these tips for your next presentation, don't be surprised when someone invites you to speak again. It will happen.